GETMORE'S GUIDE

TO MAKING MONEY

VOLUME 2

Cameron Whitmore, Mba

Disclaimer:

Cameron Whitmore is not a financial advisor. The contents of this book are for informational and entertainment purposes only and does not constitute financial, accounting or legal advice. Be sure to do your own research, and consult with professionals before making any financial decision. The author does not offer any warranty for the suggestions and contents of this book. In addition, Cameron Whitmore shall not be responsible for any losses and/or damages due to the usage of the information in this book. By reading this book, you agree to hold him harmless from any ramifications, financial or otherwise, that occur to you as a result of acting on information found in this book.

WHAT IS MONEY?

    To understand how to make money, it is important to first understand what it is, and its history. Money is just a means of exchange, and it has taken several forms over the years. No matter the currency, the transaction is always the same. One person has what another person wants, and they are willing to trade for it. Coins, paper, and crypto are only means for facilitating this trade between parties. The original format of trade was the barter, in which one item was traded for another. The challenge with bartering was finding a suitable partner to complete the trade with. The creation of currency helped to alleviate this challenge, as everyone in a region could use the same currency to buy all their goods and services. Currencies are usually managed by governments, who decide how much to produce each year depending on levels of inflation, or current state of the economy. There is an important thing to know about the American Dollar, it is considered to be Fiat Money. This means it has no instrinsic value on its own, it only has value because historically it has been used for exchange. Before 1971 the dollar was based on the gold standard, and each dollar was worth a certain amount of gold. Now instead of gold or silver certificates, Americans get Federal Reserve Notes which are legal tenders for all debts, public and private. Many countries will accept the American dollar, but most have their own unique currency such as the Euro, Peso, or Renminbi. Exchange rates change daily depending on the behavior and sentiment of the global market. Foriegn currency can be purchased at banks or airports, but most currency is exchanged daily through foreign exchanges, also known as Forex. When the dollar is strong you can buy more foriegn currency. You can use it to save up for a vacation, as a tool to save money or wait to sell the money back at a profit. Paper money is fading away in the era of digital.

    The adaptation to digital is one of the key reasons that Crypto Currency will be the preffered payment method in the future. Crypto allows people all over the world to trade their Fiat Currency for a Crypto Coin. This coin can then be sent to wallets that can be traded for other cryptos, or traded for another currency. This makes the trade between parties across the world fast, seamless and secure.

What is Crypto?

In 2009 the founder of Bitcoin, Satoshi Nakamoto, had a vision to regulate currency by math instead of governments. Crypto is not regulated by a centralized authority or government, instead it is supported by a peer to peer network that forms the block chain. The blockchain ensures all coins are tracked, showing which coins are being held in a wallet and which coins are being used in trading. This blockchain is in place to ensure that nobody can cheat the system, and many transactions require several confirmations before they are completed. The sender and reciever have to sign off on payments to make a digital signature, each person has a public and private encryption key to make this possible. There are several companies that offer wallets to hold this crypto, but be sure to pick the right one! Some wallets will happily accept your crypto to hold it, but may charge a large fee to transfer it to another account, or to exchange it for cash. The reason for this is that most transactions require some gas, or a fee to get from one location to another. The fee is usually only a fraction of ethereum, known as gwei or nanoeth, but with Ethereum currently priced over $1850, this small fraction can lead to large gas fees. Ethereum is an alternative to Bitcoin, also known as an AltCoin. Ethereum has its own blockchain platform and several other alternative coins have been built off of this platform. So now that I have reviewed the history of crypto, it is time to find out how we can make some money!

Get Your Wallet Ready

In order to hold any crypto, you must first have a wallet. As I mentioned, there are several different options, but a few wallets that I recommend using are Coinbase, Nexo Wallet or Celsius. Coinbase helps to teach you about crypto through educational videos and quizzes which reward you in Crypto! They also can reward you with crypto for "staking" your currency. Staking is similar to holding your money in a bank account. By keeping your money locked in a wallet, it helps support the network, and in exchange you can earn interest! Since you are usually rewarded in the same currency, the interest payments increase over time, unleashing the power of COMPOUND INTEREST!! Interest payments get added to the account balance, making every interest payment bigger than the one before it! Compound interest is the most powerful tool to creating wealth over time. Currently Coinbase is offering 6.0% APY to stake Algorand, 4.63% APY to stake Tezos, and 2.00% APY to stake DAI. Coinbase Pro helps to purchase crypto with much lower fees, however you have to wait a few days to verify the transaction and there is no staking of crypto. All of the crypto interest rates available are much higher than traditional banks which offer around .01% APY for most savings accounts. Some credit unions offer interest rates up to 4.0% APY for their checking accounts, but many have requirements such as direct deposit, transaction minimums, etc. Banks are a safe place to hold money by lowering the risk of it being lost or stolen, but there is also a risk to leaving money on the sidelines and not in the game. Crypto is a great way to make your money work through staking, and you can also make money by mining for Crypto using computer, laptop or mining rig.

Mining for Money

Money can many times be right underneath you. Deep under the soil there can be gold deposits, precious metals or other treasures that could be worth thousands of dollars. You can purchase a metal detector to help look for coins in your backyard, or on the beach. Sometimes creeks near rivers have small specks of gold that can be found with a gold panning kit. Some gold mines offer tours and allow you to pan on site, but this is mostly a fun hobby, and you should not expect to get rich unless you invest in heavy equipment. Another way to make mining is by mining for Crypto Currency.

Crypto Mining

To maintain the blockchain, transactions have to be verified and confirmed. This is done by various blocks being solved by using an algorithm to guess the solution. This guess is considered to be a Hash, and the more powerful your machine is the more Hash Power that you have. You can download software that helps to verify these transactions by using an algorithm that makes multiple guesses to unlock a new block and rewards everyone that helped, their portion of the reward. The more power the more of the reward is recieved. You can invest in an Application-specific integrated circuit or an ASIC, such as Antminer that is a device specifically designed to run these algorithms over and over again. You can also create a mining rig, by setting up multiple high powered GPUs to mine. If you are just getting started, you can even make money with a gaming computer. There are a few different miners, such as HoneyMiner and MinerGate, but I recommend NiceHash as the best. It offers the best return on your time and even offers a profitablity calculator to determine how much you can plan to expect to make each day from mining. A basic gaming laptop can mine about a dollar's worth of crypto each day, some powerful laptops can mine 5-10 dollars a day depending on the Graphics Processing Unit or GPU. This is the most important component in determining profitability of a mining operation. Mining usually lets off a large amount of heat due to constantly running and consuming power. You can get a mining operation setup right now using your own computer, but the pay outs will be slow and steady until there is an investment into some decent equipment. Mining is a great way to get some passive income over time, so don't expect to get rich over night.

RISK

"Scared Money Don't Make No Money." ~ Young Jeezy

    The quote about scared money is important to remember, as the main reason people do not invest is out of fear. People are afraid to invest their money, because there is a risk they will lose some or all of it. The theory is that they can avoid a loss by keeping their money in their pocket, shoebox or bank account. But in reality, this money loses value everyday. Prices tend to go up over time due to inflation, meaning the money in your pocket today will have less spending power in the future. The inflation rate in the United States is usually around 2%, so if you are not making at least 3%, you are losing money each year. It is important to put your money to work, but be sure to risk only what you can afford! Levels of risk depend on where you put your money. Bank accounts offer a safe place for your money, but they offer little return. Crypto offers a potential for huge gains, but it is an extremely volatile market with upswings and downswings, so there is a high level of risk. The riskier the transaction, the bigger the rewards usually are, but be sure to be smart about how much you are willing to risk on an investment. It is best to make small transactions consistently over time. This also provides a better cost average for the stock or currency, by purchasing them at various price points over time. Usually when people get scared, they sell their holdings to get out, but it can also be an opportunity to buy some of your favorite stocks at a discount! When a stock is soaring, it's okay to sell some. Always have a balance of safe and risky bets to diversify your investments and lower risk. Don't let fear keep you from taking action, because inaction is also a risk.

> "The greatest risk one can take is to not take risk." ~Onuh Justus Izuchukwu

HOW TO MAKE MONEY

There is an old adage that you need money to make money, but that is not entirely true. The most important thing to making money is capital. The first form of capital is human capital. This is made up of people, their experience and skillsets. A simple idea from a valuable employee can turn into a million dollar concept. We all have a value for our work, it is up to us to set that amount. Working for money is something everyone should do because it teaches the value of a dollar. The only question is how much is your time worth?

"Time is Money." ~Benjamin Franklin

Time For Money

Most people go to work everyday for a small business or corporation, they agree to trading their time for money. Employers usually set the wage during the hiring process, and determine how much they are willing to pay for an hour of work. The employee can try to negotiate for more or accept the rate through an offer letter or verbal agreement. Having and keeping a job is the most consistent way to generate income. If you need help getting a job, getting promoted, or getting a raise, I recommend reading Getmore's Guide to Success Volume 1. Many jobs offer you raises over time to reward your loyalty or your job performance. I love my career in sales as it can offer huge earning potential with commissions. There is also significant risk involved, as sales can fluctuate, and quotas or compensation plans may change over time. The only thing I can control is my amount of effort. The employees who consistently put the work in, usually have the best results, and can demand a higher salary. The goal is to be a key player on the team. Most people are comfortable in their jobs, and forget to think how much another company would be willing to pay them for their talents. Yearly raises, security and fear of the unknown, often keep talented people in their current positions. Opportunity cost is the difference from what someone could be making versus what they actually make. Your time is limited and valuable, so use it wisely. Is it you who decides the value of your time, or your company? Would another company pay you more for a similar role or position? If the answer is yes, it may be time to take the leap, update your resume, and take a risk on yourself.

Money in the Bank

After working hard and finally receiving your paycheck, the next step is to usually have this amount direct deposited into a bank account, or if your old school, go stand in line to cash the check at the bank. Having a bank account is almost a basic requirement for life. Since banks are a necessity, they can get away with offering very little return, and we still willingly send them our hard earned money. It is best to choose banks that are convenient based on availability of branches or ATMs. Banks can be national or international, while credit unions are usually regional. There are also online only banks such as Ally. These digital only banks can offer better rates due to not having to pay rent at physical branches. These are good accounts to have, but usually as a secondary since you often need to transfer from another account to the online account. If the goal is to make money from interest, the best accounts are credit unions. Credit unions are owned by their members. They use deposits to loan out money to members usually at a lower rate than banks, and share their profits in the form of higher interest rates for their checking accounts. Many of these accounts come with stipulations, so it is important to understand all the requirements to maximize your return. An important rule to learn to find out how much money you can make, is the Rule of 72. It is a calculation that tells you how long it takes for your money to double. For example if we take one of the best interest rates at about 4%, then take 72 divided by 4%, it equals 18 years for the money to double. Banks offer safety and insured deposits, but little return, great for emergency funds, but not much else.

Buy Sell or Trade

If you are looking to make some extra money, sell an item you no longer want. You can try to set a price on the item, but ultimately the value of that item is determined by how much someone is willing to pay or trade for it. What may seem like trash to one person, can be a treasure to another. There are many marketplaces that you can sell your items, Ebay, Amazon, Craigslist and Facebook to name a few. Ebay and Amazon charge fees to facilitate this trade, but they have a larger reach and there is usually no direct contact with the buyer. Anybody that has ever sold something on Craigslist or Facebook can remember having to deal with being bombarded by scammers, low ball offers and people looking for a trade. Always ask for more than you are willing to accept to leave room to negotiate. Making a deal helps both people feel better about the transaction. You can also trade items for other things you may need if cash is not needed right away. Barter only requires two people, with two items that they are willing to part with.

While Barter system has been overlooked over the years it is an effective tool. There are stories of a girl trading up from a paper clip to a car, so it is a powerful tool! If you are looking to trade, always try to make a trade for something that has a higher value than what you have to offer, and if you continue this trend you can trade up to something great over time! Just watchout for bad trades!

You can also make money with collectible items. If you have a collection, or purchase pieces of a set or series, there is a chance to find buyers that are missing the item that you have! Over the years I have had basketball card and Pokemon card collections, and it pains me to see some of the cards I had growing up selling for thousands of dollars! This is why it is important to notice trends and when something is collectible, and try to preserve it to the best of your abilities. Collectors always pay more for collectibles in pristine condition. Unopened toys and cards can demand top dollar, but you have to resist the urge of opening the package to see what is inside! If you have something really rare, it may be worth it to have it graded for its condition. Mint condition collectibles can be worth millions to the right buyer! Collecting cards, stamps, toys or coins can be a fun hobby and even make you money! Buying precious metals such as gold and silver can also be fun, but expensive. If you do not have enough to buy an ounce, there is also gold, silver and copper that can be found in coins. Pennies from 1909-1982 are 95% copper. The metal value is actually worth more than the coin itself, as according to Coinflation.com they are worth .024 cents. The site also estimates nickels from 1942-1945, aka, War Nickels, are worth $1.51 in silver or 3022% of their face value! Quarters from 1932-1964, and dimes from 1946-1964 also had silver. For the record, it is not legal to melt currency for metals, but I wanted to at least pass on the info as some coin shops will buy coins for cash. Collecting can be a fun hobby that can help you make money by selling to people with similar interests. Having an old or rare collectible can help you make money, if you are willing to let it go. Hunting for collectibles at garage and estate sales can be an adventure and also profitable with the right find.

Diversify your Income

It is important to have multiple streams of income. The impact of the coronavirus has shown us that many jobs, can be lost in an instant, and without notice. You should be prepared to make money in any situation, no matter what. Nowadays it is important to not only have a main job, but also a side hustle that can provide supplemental income. This side hustle can be a hobby such as selling collectibles, or it could be DJing house parties and weddings for your friends. My fiance Kendra recently picked up the hobby of rehabing and reselling used furniture, and her hobby has already turned into a profitable business! If you are looking to make some quick cash, you can also look into food delivery such as Uber Eats, Doordash or Postmates. These jobs offer flexibility to start and stop when you want, and also offer quick payouts if you need money in a hurry. Even with my succesful career, I am not ashamed to say I drove for Uber Eats a bit on the weekends, it is easy money and drivers can make up to $20 an hour after tips! Working multiple jobs is a great way to diversify your income, if you can maintain the grueling schedule. There were times that I had a main job throughout the day and would pick up a third shift temp job at a factory. Not only do temporary jobs offer boosts in income, working in a hot factory performing repetitive motions is a great way to lose weight and get in shape! To make money you can also offer a service to someone else for a fee. All the skills that you have gained over your lifetime have value. If you know how to work on cars, fix electronics, cut hair or do makeup, you already have a skill that can make you money! Diversification is crucial.

Get in The Market

Many of the goods and services you use everyday are owned and managed by corporations. These corportations can be privately or publicly held. If the company is publically held, anyone that purchases the stock can own a portion of the corporation. Companies issue stock as a way to raise money without having to pay interest to a lending institution or bank. Outstanding shares are the number of shares available to purchase. The total value of a company is the number of shares multiplied by the stock price, which equals the market capitalization or market cap. Companies range from nano to mega cap. A company with a stock price of $5 could be worth more than a company with a stock price of $100, all depending on the number of shares. No matter the current price of the stock today, if you purchase a share you are risking your money in hopes that the share price will increase, and the investment will be worth more in the future.

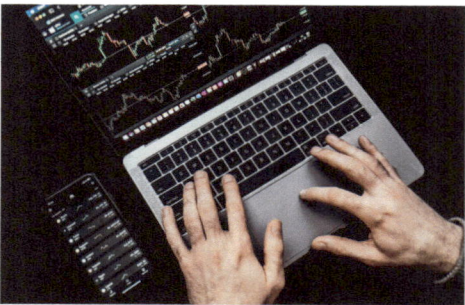

Investing is one of my favorite ways to make money, it is also volatile, and easy to lose if you don't play the game right. First I recommend finding a place to trade stocks. There are a few brokerages that now charge zero commissions for trades, while some traditional brokers charge money to buy and sell! I have tried several places, but I like to use Robinhood the most. WeBull is another great option, but I personally like Robinhood a little better for the user interface and ability to use their debit card. Use the links above to sign up and get free stocks for joining! Robinhood is still a great platform even though they got bad press for haulting trades on Gamestop and other meme stocks in 2021. I told my friends that this was actually in our best interest, and protecting the little guy. If a young novice investor decides to jump into a stock that is overbought and overpriced, they are likely to lose money quickly. Which is exactly what happened when the prices returned to normal, wiping out millions of dollars in capital in just a few days. Always remember that big money moves the market. It can be from banks or from a Reddit group pushing to drive a stock higher. When there are more buyers the stock price goes up, when there are more sellers the price of the stock goes down. With stocks, the gain or loss is not realized until they are sold, so if a stock is skyrocketing and you have doubled your investment, it's a good time to sell half and let the rest ride. Jim Cramer, the legendary investor and host of Mad Money always has one quote to live by when investing,

"Bulls and Bears make money, Pigs get slaughtered."

The goal should always be to build your account up over time. For starting traders, I recommend watching Mad Money on CNBC as Jim Cramer is a great teacher. At first I could barely understand him since he talks so fast, but over time I started to intrepret his lessons and concepts. He coaches the home gamer on how to pick stocks, and the rules of the game!

Rules of the Game

I love to play roulette. It offers the best payout if you pick the right number on each spin, but that is also the worst odds, since there are 36 numbers on the board plus 0 and 00. Casinos love the roulette table as they typically have the worst odds for the player in the house. What usually happens is a player gets lucky and wins a few spins, and then the adrenaline kicks in, and the bets increase over time. As they put down their chips you start to think, maybe 9, 12, 27, 23, 17... and then the dreaded 00s come and you lose it all.

I bring up roulette as it has many similarities to picking your investments. You can chose an individual stock such as Ford or GM, and if the price goes up, you make the most money. Other-

wise you can pick a basket of stocks such as Mutual Funds or Exchange Traded Funds (ETFs). Think about these as betting on red or black. While there is still risk, you have better odds of winning since there are more numbers in your bet. The payout is much less than playing a number straight, but it can offer steady payouts to offset the risky bets on numbers. Just as in roulette, if you are not completely sure on all the rules, it is best to stick to the basics. I recommend starting by finding some ETFs or mutual funds with low minimum requirements. This way you can get in the game without as much exposure to risk. This also helps to build your bankroll up over time.

Brokerage Accounts

Starting with your 401K at work, is a great place to start saving money. Be sure to take advantage of company match if offered, and be sure to choose which funds you want to invest in. Many accounts are defaulted to a fund with an estimated retirement date. They work by being risky in the beginning, and then becoming more conservative over time. For example, a 2025 fund will be mostly stable value, while a 2045 fund may have more growth stocks. If your account is not the way you want, most exchanges offer the ability to reallocate or rebalance your account. Companies such as Fidelity, also offer a brokerage account that can be used to pick your own individual stocks, ETF's or mutual funds. Mutual funds are a great way to get started if you can find one with low initial investment cost. I prefer type C funds as they charge a fee when the money is withdrawn, versus a type A, which charge an annual fee. I always look for type C funds that offer a monthly dividend. Companies offer a share of their profits as a reward for holding on to their investment. By reinvesting your dividends over time, you get to take advantage of compound interest, and payouts will increase over time! It also helps get a better average cost, since investing over time. If you are still afraid to do this all on your own, you can enlist the help of a professional! Financial advisors usually charge a fee to review all of your accounts and come up with a plan to make you money over time. They are a great resource, but you typically have to pay an upfront fee for the review, quarterly fees and commissions on trades. I made an investment and got an advisor and it has been good experience so far. Finding a trustworthy advisor is the best, but remember you get to make the last decision for how you want to use your money, so never feel pressured to follow all of their recommendations.

Supply and Demand

Before picking any stocks it is important to understand the rules of supply and demand. Each corportation has a certain amount of shares that is fixed. If the company set their share price at .01¢, there would be more people willing to take a chance, and invest in the company. As the price moves up, there are less people that can afford to buy a share, and are not willing to take that chance. This is why the demand curve always goes down and to the right. There are very few companies that would be willing to set their share price at .01¢, but as the share price increases there are more companies willing to part with their ownership at a higher price. This is the reason why the supply curve always goes up and to the right. When there are less shares available to buy than the market demands, a shortage is created. When there is a shortage the price always increases, because the remaining shares become more valuable. When there are more sellers than buyers in a market, a surplus is created. Sellers have to continue to lower their price, to find a potential buyer. This is exactly why stocks can have sharp price fluctuations, depending on the amount of buyers and sellers. This is usually determined by the volume of trades in a given session. High buying volume, makes share price go up, high selling volume makes a share price go down. When there is low volume there is not much movement in price at all. Day traders typically prefer stocks that have a high volume of trades to help them buy low and sell high. A Reddit group of Gamestop investors joined together, and decided to hold the stock and not sell. They called this having Diamond Hands, which meant refusing to sell their shares. When the share price skyrocketed, it was due to this low selling volume in combination with a large number of buyers that needed to cover their short position, creating a short squeeze. When an investor thinks a company is going to be worth less in the future, they will go ask a market maker if they have any shares they can sell now on their behalf and that the investor will replace them at a later time. If the investor sold 1000 shares at $10 a share, they would have $10,000. If the price goes up to $11, it would cost them an extra $1,000 to replace those shares. If the price continues to go up, their loses can continue to increase exponentially. Short sellers scramble to buy the stock at the cheapest price possible to close their short position, and end up driving up the price of the stock! A long squeeze is when investors that hold long positions sell when the market is down to cut their loses. This is what investors all saw in March 2020. People were spooked that the Coronavirus would destroy the economy, and sold their long held positions in a panic. Even though I should know better, even I did some panic selling, wiping out my long term gains to try and salvage my retirement savings. What I actually ended up doing was locking in that loss as permanent, and when the stock prices rebounded, I was not able to take advantage of those gains. I was afraid that I was going to lose it all, and by being scared, ended up missing out on a big rally. Timing the market can be difficult, but if done correctly it can be very profitable. This is why it is always best to buy consistently over time at various price levels to get the best price position. Buying shorted stocks is the new popular strategy, but it's dangerous since your up against big money. I personally like to find companies that were previously at high levels, have dropped in price and are on the rebound, but choose your own strategy.

"Buy low, Sell High." ~ Wall Street Proverb

Stock Picking

Corporations are all around us. If your just getting started, think of a product or service you really love, go to Google and add the words "stock symbol" after it and hit search. Boom! Now you have your stock symbol! This helps to research the current share price and historical data. You can look at charts that range in time from an hour, day, year or as far back to their initial public offering or IPO. Corportations make millions of shares to the public to raise money, and all shareholders own a percentage of the company! One share is only a small fraction of 1% of the company, but it still a nice feeling to have ownership in your favorite companies. Many brokerages are now allowing investors to buy partial shares, making the entire market more accessible. I like to pick stocks with a low share price, but this is risky as stocks under $10 are considered to be speculative stocks. Many institutions advise against these stocks, and prefer investment grade stocks. When looking at a low price stock try to figure out why the price is low, has it just been oversold, or is it just broken? If you can buy shares that are near their low point or bottom, you can ride with them all the way to the top! Charts typically will show a pattern over time. There are experts that follow these trends, and will purchase any company showing a certain pattern. One pattern is called Head and Shoulders. This is when there is an lift and drop in price creating a left shoulder, a large lift and drop creating the head, and followed by a lift and drop in price, creating a right shoulder. If this pattern is found in the charts, the price is likely to decrease in the future. The opposite of this pattern is known as an inverse head and shoulders, and this is a sign the stock may be due for a breakout! Remember to be careful though, as nothing is ever guaranteed. The reason big money avoids speculative stocks is because the low price could keep going down, all way to zero! Shares have to be priced at a dollar to be traded publically, so some companies perform reverse stock splits, such as giving 1 share for every 20 currently held. This can take a price from .75¢ to $15, and decreases 100 shares down to 5! A stock split lowers the price, and the shares increase. I also look for stocks that pay dividends as they can pay them, annually, semi-annually, quarterly or monthly! Stocks that pay dividends monthly are my favorite and can compound quickly when you set them to reinvest automatically. Each time the dividend is paid, the amount will increase! Once you get the dividends to a certain level, you can also use it as monthly income!

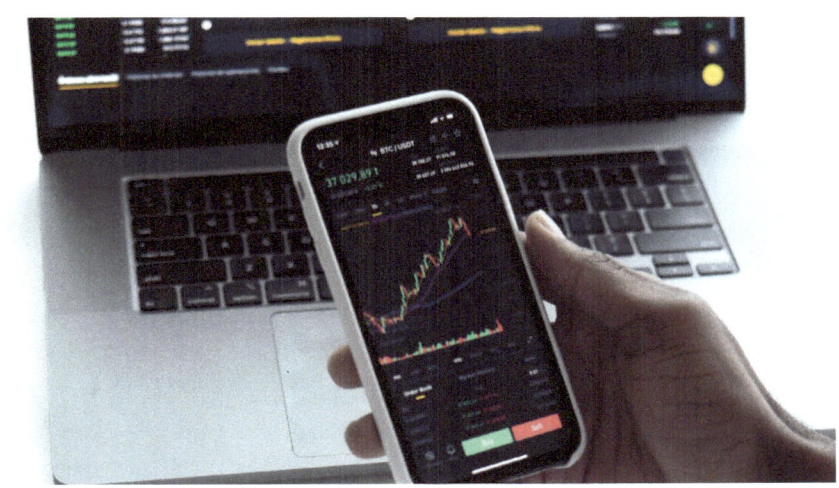

THE POWER OF CAPITAL

    The secret to success and wealth comes down to one thing, Capital. Who is willing to put their money where their mouth is, and turn their idea into reality? Most ideas never take off, mostly due to inaction. The nice thing about investing capital, is that it motivates you to take that next step, because you have something on the line. Capital is something that must be protected, as it is needed to run any business or for any investment. Human capital is the combination of skills, knowledge and work experience. A talented individual can help to increase the profits of a business, provide good financial advice, or to make a valuable team member. Having a team of smart and talented people can be more important than having money with no team. Being surrounded by the right people can help you to make more money over time, just as having the wrong people around you can cost you money. With any capital investment, there is a calculation to determine the return on that investment, or ROI, this should also be considered for human capital as well. Pick your friends and business partners wisely, as John Hope Bryant said it the best, "If you hang with 9 broke people, you'll be the 10th." Once you have a good team and idea, you can seek financial capital through business loans, grants, or competitions at local organizations. Most will require a business plan that outlines the operation of the business and how it will make money. Business plans identify team members and their roles, and also describes the plan and steps involved to getting the business off the ground. To obtain funding, there may also need to be a pitch to potential investors, so be sure your idea is fully developed. To get capital for investments, you can leverage your existing stocks to buy more shares through a margin account. These accounts usually have a minimum balance required of at least $2,000, before a margin account can be created. You can then take a margin loan against a portion of your portfolio. While this can help you to get more leverage quickly, it is still a loan that must be repaid with interest. It is also risky because if you make a bad investment, you may have to sell your long term positions to cover your margin loan. Capital is needed to make a return, but choose your sources of capital wisely. All you need is a good idea, a good plan, a good team and some initial capital, and you can make money in almost any business.

Stay away from the WILD Card

One phrase that I remember from a book I once read, was that you should never try to get rich using a WILD card. The W stands for welfare. Being on welfare never truly helps anyone to get rich, as they want to keep you at a certain pay level forever, or risk losing benefits. It's crazy to think that someone working two jobs to try to provide for their family, would have their benefits cut because they were over a maximum threshold. While I was in college, I had to work two jobs and was only offered $10 per month in food assistance. Of course to stay in the program, I had to answer very invasive questions, have a case worker, and constantly update them. Welfare is not designed to help you get rich, it is designed to help keep you poor. The I in WILD Card is for Insurance. While insurance payouts help provide for family members after a loss in the family, this should not be relied on to get you rich. Some people may also try to scam insurance companies with fraudulent claims, which is another bad idea, as employees are trained to spot any fraud. The L in WILD Card is for Lottery. I know buying scratch offs at the gas station is fun and can be addictive, but it is the worst investment for your money you can make. When you scratch off that losing ticket, you might as well have burned your money since it's gone. Powerball and Mega Millions aren't any better since the odds of winning are so low, and with all the different combinations, Pick 3 or 4 aren't the best either. The D in WILD Card is for Drugs. Movies and videos show gangsters flashing thousands of dollars that they earned selling drugs, but this is not only an illegal profession, it is dangerous, and it can kill you.

The Value of a Dollar

To most people a dollar isn't much money, but it is important to never forget the value of a dollar! Even a million dollars has to start at one, and if you learn how to earn one dollar, the technique and effort can be multiplied several times and eventually lead to great wealth. The goal of this book was to help you to make at least one dollar, and if you do, then my mission is complete. I am not a certified financial advisor, so please take my advice with a grain of salt, but I feel we can all learn something from each other. Never forget the things a dollar can buy for you such as food, water, or gas. That is exactly why casinos like you to trade in your money for chips, or a deposit slip at a slot machine, because then the money does not seem as real. It is easy to forget that black chip is worth a hundred dollars, and could fill your tank a few times, or buy food for a week. The same can be said of stocks and other investments. Replacing your money with stock symbols can make it all seem like a game, but never lose sight of the cost to play. If you make a profit, it is okay to earn a few dollars, a profit in any amount is always a win! The goal is to get in the game as soon as possible to put your money to work and to take advantage of time. The power of compounding interest and dividend payments will help grow your money over time, and make your money work for you while you sleep! Once you figure out how to put your money to work, you become one step closer to financial freedom. Be smart and make good investments, so later you can enjoy your riches and do what you want to do in life.

Links and Photo Credits

Robinhood Referral Link

https://join.robinhood.com/camerow589

Nexo Referral Link

https://nexo.io/?u=601dfc3aeea4d00cd447a212

Coins and Crypto. David Mcbee, Pexels.

Banknote Lot. Pixabay, Pexels.

U.S. Dollar Banknote Lot. Pixabay, Pexels.

Heap of different nominal per dollars. Karolina Grabowska. Pexels.

Person Using Macbook Pro on White Table. Alesia Kozik. Pexels

Roulette. Anna Shvets. Pexels.

Chips, Dice, Cards. Pixabay. Pexels.

Stocks with Phone in Hand. Anna Nekrashevich. Pexels

100 US Dollar Banknotes on Cover. John Guccione. Pexels.

www.ingramcontent.com/pod-product-compliance
Lightning Source LLC
Chambersburg PA
CBHW040305220526
45473CB00002B/589